WHISPER AND SHOUT

Written by
KATE RUTTLE

Illustrated by
CHARLOTTE COOKE

WAYLAND

First published in 2011
by Wayland

Text copyright © Kate Ruttle 2011

Illustration copyright © Wayland 2011

Wayland
338 Euston Road
London NW1 3BH

Wayland Australia
Level 17/207 Kent Street
Sydney, NSW 2000

Series editor: Louise John
Editor: Katie Woolley
Designer: Paul Cherrill
Consultant: Kate Ruttle

A CIP catalogue record for this book is available
from the British Library.

ISBN 9780750263900

Printed in China

Wayland is a division of Hachette Children's Books,
an Hachette UK company. www.hachette.co.uk

Fizz Wizz Phonics is a series of fun and exciting books, especially designed to be used by children who have not yet started to read.

The books support the development of language, exploring key speaking and listening skills, as well as encouraging confidence in pre-reading skills.

WHISPER AND SHOUT is all about voice sounds. We can make our voices high or low, and we can speak quickly and slowly. We can also use our voices to show action or feeling, such as "Aaaaaargh" and requests like "Sssshh". This book tells the story of Jake and Ella's birthday, beginning with the twins opening their presents to having fun playing hide and seek with their friends. Throughout the story children will explore the sounds we can make when making different mouth movements, such as blowing, sucking and stretching.

For suggestions on how to use **WHISPER AND SHOUT** and for further activities, look at page 24 of this book.

In the Bedroom

Early one morning, Jake and Ella burst into Mum and Dad's bedroom.

They were very excited
as it was their birthday.
"Yippee!" they shouted.

The Pile of Presents

Just then Jake spotted a pile
of presents.
"Are those for us?" he squealed.
"Oooo," whispered Ella.

Jake and Ella began to rip open the paper to see what was inside each parcel.

Breakfast

Then it was time for breakfast. Jake and Ella ate quickly, as they wanted to play with their new toys!

"This train is my favourite," said Ella.
"Ch, ch, chooo."
"I like this car best!" said Jake.
"Nee nor, nee nor, nee nor!"

A Birthday Party

That afternoon, Jake and Ella's friends came over to play. They all played the farmyard game. It was very noisy!

"Woof! Woof!" barked Ella.
"Quack! Quack!" yelled Jake.
"Meow!" cried Lami.
"Moo!" shouted Sam.

Hide and Seek

vroom

Jake was soon bored of the
farmyard game. He wanted to play
hide and seek. Jake ran off to hide.

Sam and Lami couldn't find him
anywhere. At last Mum and Ella
spotted Jake under the bed.
"Sssh, there he is," whispered Mum.

In the Garden

Then Jake, Ella and their
friends went outside to play.
"Whee!" shouted Ella, as she slid
down the slide.

"Watch out, Jake!" shouted Mum.
But Jake tripped and hurt his knee.
"Ouch!" he cried.

Time for Tea

Soon it was time for Jake and Ella's birthday tea. There was pizza, sandwiches, cakes and fruit.

Jake forgot about his sore knee
when he saw all of the food.
"Oooo," whispered Jake.

Birthday Cake

Suddenly, the lights went out. Ella looked around and saw Mum carrying the biggest cake she'd ever seen! "Wow," gasped Jake and Ella.

Everyone sang "Happy Birthday"
to Jake and Ella. Then they took
a big breath and they blew out
all of the candles.

Going Home

After tea, all the mums
and dads came to take
the children home.

Ella and Jake gave their friends
a slice of cake in a little bag.
"Goodbye!" shouted Jake and Ella.

Time for Bed

As soon as everyone had gone, it was time for bed. Jake and Ella were feeling very sleepy.
"Goodnight," whispered Mum and Dad.

It didn't take long for Jake and Ella to fall asleep. That night they both dreamt about the best birthday ever.

Further Activities

 These activities can be used when reading the book one-to-one, or in the home.

 These activities can be used when using the book with more than one child, or in an educational setting.

P4 • Look at the picture and read the story on this page. What might the family be saying to one another? Some examples might be "Happy birthday" and "Good morning".

P6 • Talk about the noises that might be heard in this picture, including the sound of ripping paper, the sound the camera makes and the noises the children might be making.
• Can you imitate these noises with your own voice?

P8 • Jake and Ella are busy playing with their toys. Talk about the sounds each toy makes. Can you think of other noises the toys might make?
• What kind of sounds might the children make as they play with their toys?

P10 • How many animal noises do you know? Which is your favourite?
• Talk about the noises each child in the picture is making.

P12 • Can you make the same sound that Mum is making in this picture? When is it appropriate to use that sound?

P14 • Look at all of the children playing in the picture. Try to copy the noises each child is making. Who's crying? Who's laughing? Talk about why they're making these noises.

P16 • Make a picnic lunch with some crisps, cucumber, raw carrot and cheese. Listen to the sounds you make as you eat. Which foods are noisy and which are quiet?

P18 • The story says Jake and Ella 'gasped'. What kind of noise is that? Can you make the noise? Do you know when you would make that noise?
• What other sounds are in this picture?

P20 • Look at the picture and talk about where it would be noisy or quiet to walk. Is the gravel path noisy or quiet? How about the grass?
• Go for a walk outside and listen to the sounds your footsteps make on different surfaces. Are they noisy or quiet?

P22 • Are people always quiet when they sleep? Can you mimic some of the sounds people might make in their sleep?

P4 • Talk about the sounds you might hear in the room, for example is the cat purring? Can you make a sound like a cat purring?
• What sound is made when Jake kisses Mum?

P6 • Rip up a newspaper and listen to the sound it makes. Can you make that same noise with your voice?

P8 • Make a collection of noisy toys such as a jack-in-the-box, a toy car and a talking doll. Talk about how and why each one makes a noise.
• Mimic the noises of one of the toys above. Can your friends guess which toy you are imitating?

P10 • As a group, play Ella's farmyard game. Stick a picture of a different animal on each child's back. Only that child will know which animal they are. Take it in turns to make the noise of your animal and see if your friends can guess what animal you are!

P12 • As a group, think of a list of sounds people might make as they play hide and seek.

P14 • Look at the picture and think about loud voice noises and soft voice noises. Mum shouted, "Watch out Jake". Was that soft or loud? Can you demonstrate how she might have said the words?

P16 • Think of some words to describe the noises that you might hear around a party table, for example 'crunch', 'slurp', 'squirt' and 'mmmm'.

P18 • Reread the book and try to listen out for words which tell you how people spoke or the noises they made, for example 'shouted' on page 4, 'cried' on page 15 and 'gasped' on page 18.
• Do you know any other words that describe how people speak?

P20 • Talk about what each of the people in the picture might be saying. You could try to use some of the describing words you found when doing the activity on page 18–19.
• What other sounds might there be in this picture?

P22 • Make a picture map showing what Ella and Jake did on their birthday. How much do you remember? Work as a group to remember or think of words and sounds that accompany each stage of Jake and Ella's birthday.